Picture Reference

TRANSPORT

● ● ● ● ● ● ● ● ● ● ● ● ● ●

DAVID GLOVER

How to use this book

Contents
The contents page at the front of the book lists the main subjects in the book and on which pages you can find them.

Cross-references
Above the heading on the page, you will find a list of subjects that are related to the topic. These subjects are listed with their page numbers. Turn to these pages to find out more about each subject.

Glossary words
Difficult words are explained in the glossary on page 46. These words are written in **bold**. Look them up in the glossary to find out what they mean.

Index
The index is on pages 47–48. It is a list of important words mentioned in the book in alphabetical order, with the page numbers written next to them. If you want to read about a subject, look it up in the index, then turn to the page number given.

Titles in this series
Atlas
Space
Animals
Transport

Created and published by
Two-Can Publishing Ltd
346 Old Street
London
EC1V 9NQ

Art director: Belinda Webster
Managing editor: Deborah Kespert
Senior designer: Helen Holmes
Commissioning editor: Julia Hillyard
Editorial support: Flavia Bertolini, Amanda Nathan, Robert Sved
Picture research: Laura Cartwright
Consultant: John Becklake
Main illustrations: Nick Hawken
Computer illustrations: Mel Pickering

Hardback ISBN 1-85434-602-4
Paperback ISBN 1-85434-618-0

Dewey Decimal Classification 388

Hardback 2 4 6 8 10 9 7 5 3 1
Paperback 2 4 6 8 10 9 7 5 3 1

A catalogue record for this book is available from the British Library.

Photographic credits:
B & C Alexander p42, p43br; Britstock-IFA/Bernd Ducke p5, p13, p16, B-IFA p17tl; Image Bank/Leo Mason p9, IB/Paolo Curto p19tl, IB/Andy Caulfield p20, IB/Guido A Rossi p35tl; James Davis Travel Photography p12; Japan Marine Science & Technology Center p33; NASA/Science Photo Library p35br; Pictor International p15, p25c; Pictures Colour Library p27; Powerstock Photo Library/A Gin p7br, p25t; Quadrant Picture Library/Anthony R Dalton p17br; Rick Tomlinson p19c; Robert Harding Picture Library/Christopher Rennie p24, RHPL/Ron Behrmann p34; Tony Stone Images/Lori Adamski Peek p7tl, TSI/Mark Joseph p11, TSI/Paul Chesley p23, TSI p28, TSI/James Balog p29, TSI/Mike Sarowiak p37, TSI/Arnulf Husmo p39, TSI/David R Frazier p43t.

Printed and bound in Spain by Graficas Reunidas

Contents

How do people travel?   4

Cycles and skates   6

Motorcycle   8

Car   10

Truck   12

Road   14

Bus and tram   16

Emergency vehicles   18

Train   20

Underground train   22

Travelling on water   24

Ferry   26

Working boats   28

Harbour   30

Underwater boats   32

Travelling in the air   34

Aeroplane   36

Helicopter   38

Airport   40

Travelling on snow   42

Amazing facts   44

Glossary   46

Index   47

How do people travel?

For thousands of years, the only way that we could travel from one place to another was by walking or riding animals. Since then, we have discovered faster ways of moving around. Bicycles, cars, buses and trains carry us over the land, while ships take us across the oceans. We also fly through the air in huge aeroplanes and can even travel into space and back.

▶ Camels are perfect for carrying people and goods long distances across hot deserts. They have wide feet which do not sink into the sand.

Changing transport

This timeline shows important inventions that have changed the way people travel.

Wheel about 3500 BC	**Sailing boat** about 3000 BC	**Hot-air balloon** 1783	**Steam train** 1825

Nobody knows who invented the wheel, but an ancient people, called the Sumerians, were the first people to attach it to carts pulled by oxen.	The ancient Egyptians were the first people to invent sailing boats. They made them from planks of wood, then added sails to drive them across the water.	People were first carried into the air by hot-air balloons. Two French brothers, Joseph and Jacques Montgolfier, built the first successful hot-air balloon.	An Englishman called George Stephenson designed the first train to carry passengers. It was driven by steam and had a top speed of 24 km per hour.

► Towns are often packed with cars, buses, vans and other **vehicles**. Too many vehicles can cause noise, traffic jams and **pollute** the air.

Motorcar
1885

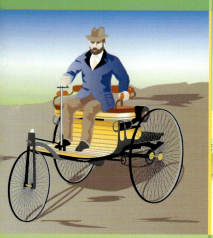

A German called Karl Benz built the first motorcar. It looked like a three-wheeled bicycle but it was powered by an **engine** that burned **petrol**.

Aeroplane
1903

The Americans Wilbur and Orville Wright built the first successful aeroplane, The Flyer. On its first flight, it flew just 36 m and was in the air for 12 seconds.

Space rocket
1961

In 1961, a Russian space rocket sent the first person into space. In 1969, two Americans landed on the Moon. They travelled in the rocket shown above.

Space shuttle
1981

Space shuttles were the first **spacecraft** that could be reused. On board, a crew of **astronauts** carries out repairs and experiments in space.

Cycles and skates

Cycles and skates are **vehicles** with wheels that you power with your legs. They are cheap to run and repair and they do not have **engines** that **pollute** the air. In 1839, in Scotland, the first two-wheeled cycle with pedals was built. It was called a bicycle. Today, all over the world, millions of people ride bicycles. Cycling is faster than walking and it keeps people fit and healthy.

Bicycle
This boy is riding a mountain bicycle. It has a tough **steel** frame and chunky tyres for cycling over rough land. As the boy rides, he uses his leg **muscles** to push round the pedals. This moves a chain which turns the back wheel.

helmet
The cyclist wears a helmet to protect his head.

tyre
Inside the thick rubber tyre, there is a tube pumped full of air.

gears
This bicycle has several **gears**. Changing to a lower gear makes it easier to cycle uphill.

chain

pedal

handlebars
The cyclist controls the brakes and gears from here. The handlebars also help him to steer the bicycle.

brakes
When the cyclist brakes, these brake pads rub against the wheels and stop the bicycle.

Rollerblades

Travelling on rollerblades is great fun and good exercise. You can practise tricks in the park or quickly slip past walkers on your way home. This skater is wearing knee and elbow pads, gloves and a crash helmet to protect her body if she falls.

Racing bicycle

A lightweight racing bicycle zooms along at high speed. It has smooth narrow tyres which roll easily along the road. The rider holds on to special upright grips on her handlebars and leans forwards into the wind. A **streamlined** helmet and tight clothes help her to cut smoothly through the rushing air.

Skateboarding

A skateboard has four roller-skate wheels fixed to a board. You need good balance to stand on the board and scoot along. Skateboarders practise on special tracks. Expert skateboarders can leap, twist and even somersault without falling over.

Rickshaw

This three-wheeled cycle is called a rickshaw. In many Asian countries, passengers pay rickshaw drivers to take them across town. It is hard work for the driver, particularly in hot weather. Rickshaws are popular in crowded cities because they are a cheap type of transport and can squeeze through traffic jams.

Go to Cycles and skates page 6, Travelling on snow page 42

Motorcycle

A motorcycle has two wheels and an **engine** fixed to a strong frame. Travelling by motorcycle is a fast and easy way to move around. A rider can dart through traffic jams and squeeze into small parking spaces. Riding a motorcycle is exciting and fun, but to be safe, riders must wear tough leather clothes and a helmet. These protect them if they fall off and keep them warm and dry as they speed along.

windscreen
The windscreen helps to make the motorcycle more **streamlined** by pushing rushing air over the top of the rider. .....

Trail bike
A trail bike is built for riding off-road. It can travel along country trails, climb hills and even cross streams. It has thick tyres for extra grip.

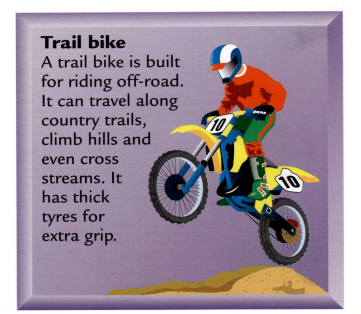

headlamp ....
At night, a bright headlamp lights the road ahead and lets other drivers know that the motorcycle is coming.

Motor scooter
A motor scooter is perfect for riding in cities. It has small wheels and a comfortable platform for the rider's feet. It is cheaper and easier to ride than a full-size motorcycle.

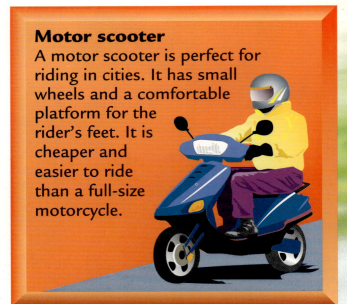

treads ....
In wet weather, grooves in the tyres, called treads, push away rainwater. This helps to stop the motorcycle from skidding.

wing mirror
Before overtaking, the rider checks her wing mirrors to see if there are any **vehicles** behind.

Motorcycle racing
Motorcycle racing is a thrilling, risky sport. To balance their bikes around the bends, the riders lean over until their knees almost touch the ground.

fuel tank
Petrol is stored in the **fuel** tank. To fill the tank, the rider unscrews a cap and pours in the petrol.

pannier
Containers, called panniers, are useful for carrying tools and extra clothes.

Factfile
The world's smallest working motorcycle is about 10 cm high and 15 cm long. It is so small that it can even stand on a saucer.

The first motorcycle was built in 1885 by Gottfried Daimler. It was made of wood with a petrol engine.

In 1991, Yasuyuki Kudo rode on one wheel of his motorcycle for 331 km.

engine
An engine which burns **petrol** powers the motorcycle.

gear lever
To change **gear**, the rider pushes the gear lever up or down with her foot.

Go to Emergency vehicles page 18, Road page 14

Car

In many countries, the car is the most popular way of travelling. The first cars, built just over 100 years ago, were noisy, slow and often broke down. Modern cars are more reliable and much faster. They are designed to be comfortable for both long and short journeys. But today, in many cities, there are too many cars that create long traffic jams and **pollute** the air.

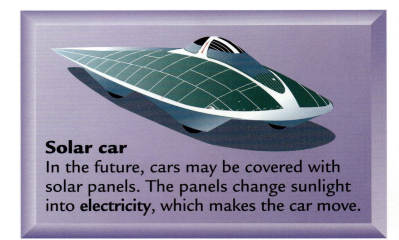

Solar car
In the future, cars may be covered with solar panels. The panels change sunlight into **electricity**, which makes the car move.

steering wheel
The driver uses the steering wheel to turn the wheels to the left or right.

dashboard
Lights and dials on the dashboard show the car's speed and the amount of petrol in the tank.

engine
The **engine** is usually at the front of the car, under the bonnet. It burns **petrol** and makes the wheels move round.

pedals
To go faster, the driver pushes the accelerator pedal. This sends more petrol to the engine. The brake pedal slows down the car.

seatbelt
The driver and passengers wear seatbelts to protect themselves if they are in an accident.

brake
When the driver presses the brake pedal, pads inside the wheels push down to stop the car.

Built by robots
Cars are made up of hundreds of parts which are put together in a factory. Sparks fly as **robots** fix the parts on to the body of each car. A new car is completed every few minutes.

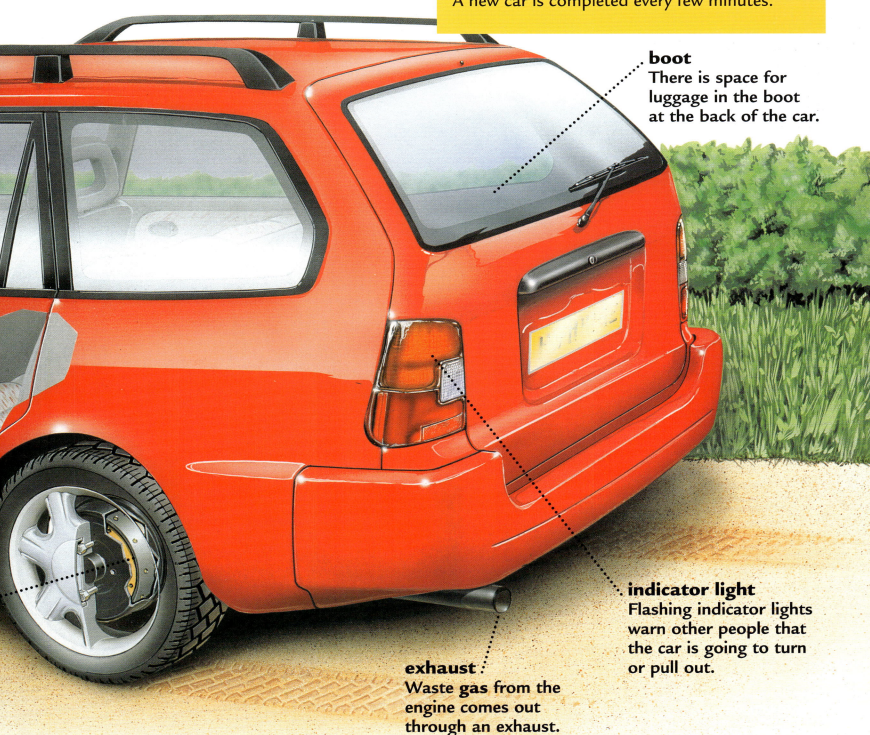

boot
There is space for luggage in the boot at the back of the car.

indicator light
Flashing indicator lights warn other people that the car is going to turn or pull out.

exhaust
Waste **gas** from the engine comes out through an exhaust.

Go to Emergency vehicles page 18, Road page 14, Travelling on snow page 42

Truck

A truck is a large **vehicle** that carries goods from place to place. It may take the goods from one part of town to another or drive for days from one country to another. Trucks have powerful **engines**, which run on **diesel**, to pull their heavy loads. Many trucks are built to do special tasks, such as heave materials around a building site.

Driver's cab
On long journeys, the cab is the driver's home. It is roomy and comfortable with a bed at the back for sleeping.

Articulated truck

Most large trucks are articulated, which means that they are made up of two parts that hook together. This allows the truck to turn corners more easily. The front section, called a tractor, has a powerful engine and driver's cab. It hauls a long trailer loaded with goods.

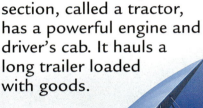

tractor
The tractor easily unhooks so that it can pull different kinds of trailers.

trailer
This refrigerated trailer keeps fruit or meat fresh on the way to the supermarket.

Road train

A road train is a long truck that transports goods to places where there are no railways. Its powerful engine pulls several heavy trailers over long distances. This road train is carrying two enormous tankfuls of **petrol** all the way across Australia. Underneath, it has 42 wheels to support its heavy load.

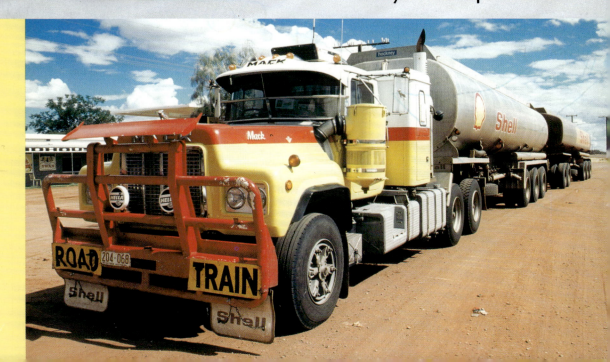

Building roads

Modern trucks work together to build new roads as quickly as possible. Each truck has its own job and carries out the work of hundreds of people with shovels. Some trucks clear the ground, dig ditches, or carry away soil, while others deliver building materials, such as cement or pipes. Enormous tyres help the trucks to move over the rough ground.

digger

A digger has a long arm with sharp teeth for cutting out ditches. It moves on **caterpillar tracks**.

cement truck

Wet cement is mixed in the spinning drum of a cement truck. It pours out of the truck through a chute.

loader

A loader shovels up loose soil and carries it away in a large bucket.

Refuse truck

A refuse truck takes rubbish from outside your home to the dump. A lift at the back of the truck picks up a rubbish bin and empties it into the trailer. Inside, a ram squashes the rubbish down. When the truck reaches the dump, the trailer tips up and the rubbish tumbles out.

Fork-lift truck

Fork-lift trucks shift heavy boxes and crates around a warehouse. The boxes rest in piles on flat pieces of wood called pallets. The driver just slides the truck's two long forks through a pallet and pushes a lever inside the cab to lift the boxes up.

Go to Car page 10, Travelling on snow page 42, Truck page 12

Road

Long roads cut across most countries, linking towns and cities along the way. Roads make it easy for people to travel quickly from one place to another. The first roads were rough, muddy and narrow but today, in most places, they are much wider and smoother with sloping sides for rainwater to drain away.

▶ Near cities, small roads link up with wide, high-speed roads called motorways.

motorway
On a motorway, cars can travel at up to 110 km per hour.

hard shoulder
In an emergency, drivers pull off the motorway on to the hard shoulder, to wait for help.

slip road
A slip road gives **vehicles** leaving the motorway plenty of room to slow down.

lane
A motorway has several lanes. Drivers use two of the lanes for overtaking slower vehicles.

Cats'-eyes are pieces of glass on the lines of lanes, which reflect a car's headlights. At night, they help drivers to see where they are going.

Signs help to keep road users safe. There are many different kinds, including ones which tell the fastest safe speed to travel.

Traffic lights control the traffic at junctions. Red tells drivers to stop, amber shows that the lights are about to change and green means go.

tunnel
It is much faster to drive through a tunnel than around or over a mountain.

bypass
Many vehicles avoid the busy city centre by driving round it on a bypass.

flyover
A flyover is built above another road, so that cars can pass quickly without stopping.

junction
A junction is where two or more roads meet. Drivers can turn on to another road at a junction.

Getting across
A bridge is a quick way for traffic to cross rivers, valleys and railways. The Golden Gate Bridge in the United States is almost 3 km long. It is held up by cables that loop down from towers.

Factfile

The longest traffic jam in history took place in 1980, outside Lyon in France. It was 176 km long, which is the length of 44,000 cars standing bumper to bumper!

Spaghetti Junction, in England, is a famous tangle of roads that cross each other in one place. Eighteen roads meet on six different levels.

Go to Road page 14, Train page 20

Bus and tram

A bus carries many passengers at a time along set **routes**. It takes them on long journeys across country as well as short city trips. Many years ago, buses were pulled by horses but, today, most buses have large **engines** that use **diesel**. Trams are similar to buses but they run on rails through the city streets and are powered by **electricity**. Travelling by bus and tram saves **fuel** and reduces traffic on roads.

Chugging along
This bright red London bus is a double-decker. Passengers travel on two levels, called the upper and lower **decks**. On some buses, a conductor collects the fares while the driver sits in the cab, concentrating on the traffic.

City bus
A ride on a modern city bus is quiet and smooth. Passengers buy their tickets in advance from the ticket office or a machine, or they pay on board. Along the route, large **automatic** doors slide open at stops so that people can climb on and off the bus.

bell
Passengers ring a bell to let the driver know that they want to get off at the next stop.

bus station
The bus begins its journey at a bus station. People wait under shelters for their buses to arrive.

School bus

Many children live too far from their school to walk there and back so, on school days, they may travel on special buses to the school grounds. Flashing lights or signs at the back of the bus warn other drivers to slow down as the children climb on and off.

Crowded bus

In countries where there are few cars, the only way to travel may be by bus. This bus is packed with people taking their goods to market. When the bus is full up inside, sacks, buckets and even animals are piled high on the roof.

destination plate

A destination plate with a number shows where the bus is going.

Tram

Many towns and cities have trams as well as buses. Trams run on **steel** tramlines set into the road. A metal frame on the roof, called a pantograph, powers the tram by picking up electricity from overhead cables. Trams have been used since 1880, but when cars and buses became more common, many tramlines were torn up to make way for wider roads. Recently, trams have become popular again, because they **pollute** the air less than buses.

Go to Airport page 40, Ferry page 26, Helicopter page 38, Working boats page 28

Emergency vehicles

In an emergency, people need help quickly, so special **vehicles** speed to the rescue. Flashing lights and wailing sirens tell you that they are on their way. These vehicles are designed for different jobs and carry the latest equipment. The men and women who operate them are highly trained.

Fire engine

Fire engines carry huge ladders and long hoses to the scene of a blaze. The ladder on the back of this fire engine can be lengthened to lift the firefighter high into the air, either to rescue a person or to shoot a powerful jet of water into the flames.

water supply
Water is pumped from a fire hydrant or from a tank in the fire engine.

safety cage
A firefighter stands in the safety cage at the top of the ladder to put out the flames.

turntable
The long ladder swivels into position on a turning base called a turntable.

outriggers
The outrigger legs keep the fire engine level while the ladder is raised.

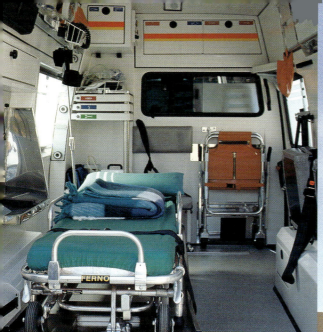

Police car

A police car is often the first vehicle to arrive at a traffic accident. Warning lights and reflective stripes make sure that it can be seen easily by day or night. This policeman is using his car radio to call for other emergency services to bring more help.

Ambulance

When a person has an accident, or suddenly becomes unwell, an ambulance may take them to hospital. Inside the ambulance, there are warm blankets, a bed on wheels called a stretcher, and plenty of first aid equipment to treat the patient immediately.

Lifeboat

A lifeboat rescues people in trouble at sea. It carries floats and lifebelts that the crew throws to people in the water to help them to safety. It also has medical and firefighting equipment on board. Although lifeboats are small, they are made of tough plastic that can survive the roughest seas. This modern lifeboat is self-righting, which means that if the boat turns over in a storm, it will flip the right way up again by itself.

Breakdown truck

When your car breaks down, you can use a telephone to call for a breakdown truck. If the truck driver cannot mend the car, he or she will attach it to the back of the truck and tow it to a garage. Breakdown trucks need to be sturdy to pull heavy vehicles and to work in the rain or snow.

Go to Bus and tram page 16, Underground train page 22

Train

A train is a line of carriages pulled along a railway track by a special car called a locomotive. Most locomotives use **diesel** or **electricity** to move. Trains carry passengers and goods quickly and safely between towns and cities. On many modern trains, passengers on long journeys can eat in the restaurant car, make telephone calls and even sleep overnight in sleeping carriages.

All around the world
This powerful train uses diesel to run its electric motors. Diesel-electric trains were first developed in the 1950s. Today, they are the most common type of train in the world.

▼ This modern train is powered entirely by electricity. It shoots across the land at speeds of up to 300 km per hour.

pantograph
A frame, called a pantograph, picks up electricity from overhead cables.

driver's cab
In the cab, the driver uses a radio to keep in touch with controllers in railway stations along the way.

power car
The locomotive pulling this train is called a power car. It uses electricity from the overhead cables to run the **motors**.

electric motor
Electric motors behind these springs turn the wheels.

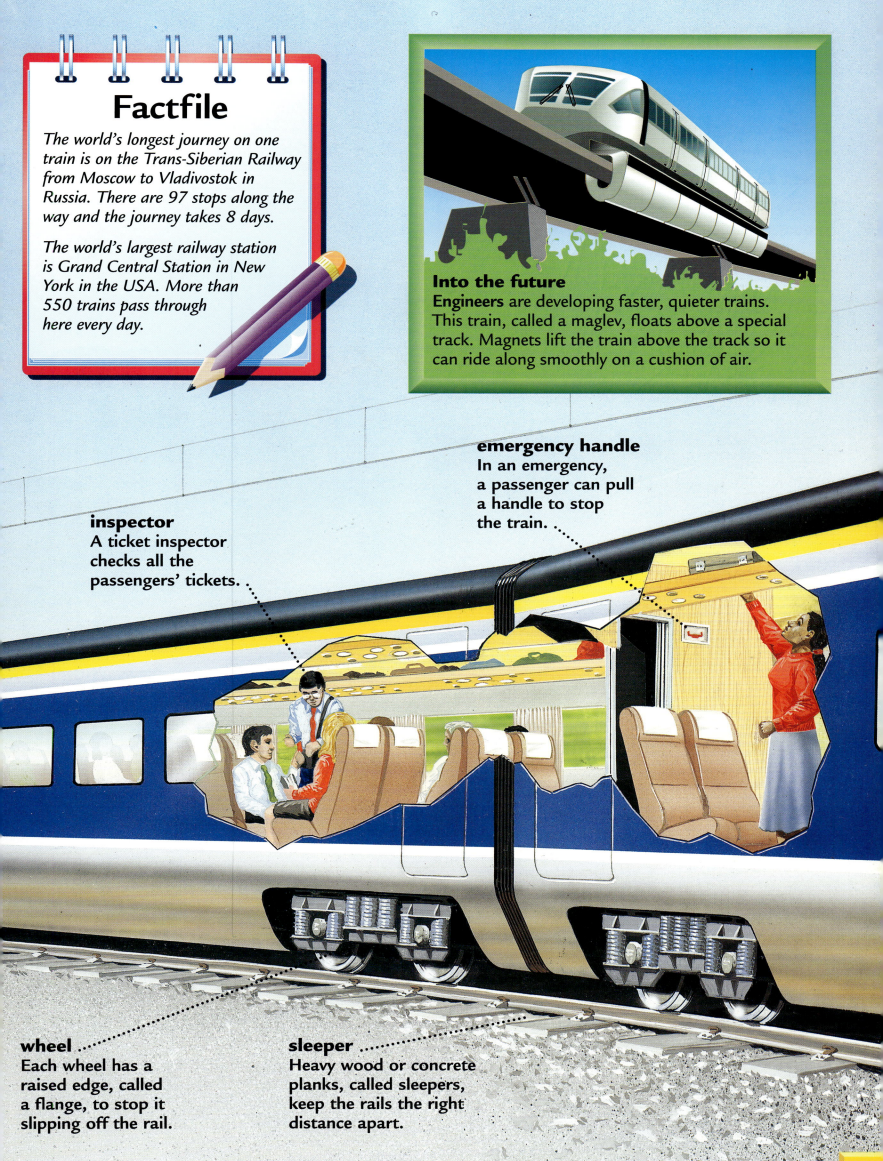

Factfile

The world's longest journey on one train is on the Trans-Siberian Railway from Moscow to Vladivostok in Russia. There are 97 stops along the way and the journey takes 8 days.

The world's largest railway station is Grand Central Station in New York in the USA. More than 550 trains pass through here every day.

Into the future
Engineers are developing faster, quieter trains. This train, called a maglev, floats above a special track. Magnets lift the train above the track so it can ride along smoothly on a cushion of air.

emergency handle
In an emergency, a passenger can pull a handle to stop the train.

inspector
A ticket inspector checks all the passengers' tickets.

wheel
Each wheel has a raised edge, called a flange, to stop it slipping off the rail.

sleeper
Heavy wood or concrete planks, called sleepers, keep the rails the right distance apart.

Go to Train page 20

Underground train

Underground trains run through tunnels beneath city streets. Every day, in busy cities such as London, New York and Paris, hundreds of thousands of people travel on underground trains to go shopping or to travel to school or work. Entrances at street level lead passengers down to the stations, deep below the ground. Their trains arrive regularly, every few minutes.

▶ This picture shows the different levels of an underground railway station hidden beneath the streets.

station entrance
Stairs lead down from the station entrance into the main hall.

TICKETS

TICKETS

ticket machine
You buy your ticket from a machine or a ticket seller.

barrier
An **automatic** barrier checks your ticket before letting you through.

arrival display
The arrival display tells you when the next train arrives and where it goes.

NEXT TRAIN
5 MINUTES

train
An underground train arrives with a rush of air. It runs on an **electric** rail.

automatic door
You climb on and off the train through the sliding automatic doors.

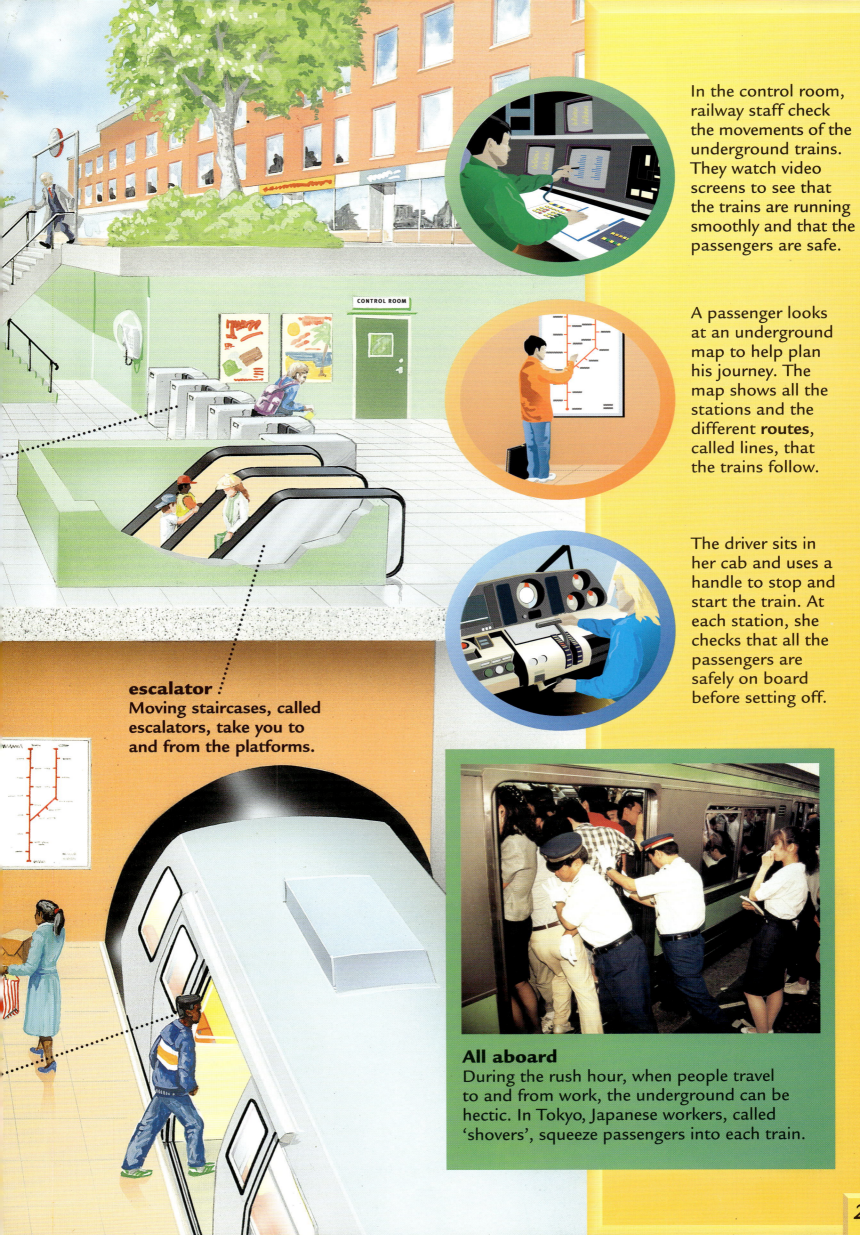

CONTROL ROOM

In the control room, railway staff check the movements of the underground trains. They watch video screens to see that the trains are running smoothly and that the passengers are safe.

A passenger looks at an underground map to help plan his journey. The map shows all the stations and the different **routes**, called lines, that the trains follow.

The driver sits in her cab and uses a handle to stop and start the train. At each station, she checks that all the passengers are safely on board before setting off.

escalator
Moving staircases, called escalators, take you to and from the platforms.

All aboard
During the rush hour, when people travel to and from work, the underground can be hectic. In Tokyo, Japanese workers, called 'shovers', squeeze passengers into each train.

Go to Ferry page 26, Harbour page 30, Working boats page 28

Travelling on water

Small boats were one of the first kinds of transport to be invented. People powered these early boats by using their arms to move poles, paddles and oars through the water. Later, they added sails so that the wind moved the boat along. Today, huge **cargo** ships and passenger liners, driven by massive **diesel engines**, sail to and fro across the great oceans.

mast
The mast holds up the sails. This one is as high as a four-storey house.

Reed boat
For thousands of years, people have used natural **materials** found nearby to build boats. On Lake Titicaca, in the mountains of South America, local people build fishing canoes from reeds that grow on the banks of the lake.

sail ....
Yacht sails are triangular with a curved outside edge.

crew
The crew wears life jackets to keep them afloat in case they fall overboard in rough weather.

Sailing yacht
The tall sails of a modern yacht catch the wind and power the boat across the waves. The clever sail design means that a yacht can move in any direction apart from straight into the wind. Large racing yachts take part in long ocean races, sometimes travelling all the way round the world.

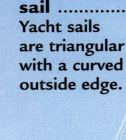

rudder
To help steer the boat, the crew moves a rudder. ....

Ocean liner

Before the age of huge passenger aeroplanes, people travelled the world on ocean liners. It took about four days to sail from London to New York, a journey that now takes seven hours by aeroplane. Today, liners are mostly used for holiday cruises. The body of an ocean liner is made of metal, which is heavier than water. It floats because the **hull** is full of air, which is lighter than the water around it.

Life on board

An ocean liner is a luxurious hotel on water. It has everything a passenger needs. On the sun **deck**, passengers relax by the swimming pool. Afterwards they can play sport and visit restaurants or cinemas, before going to sleep in their comfortable cabins.

Speedboat

A speedboat skims lightly over the surface of the water at up to 65 km per hour, which is as fast as a car on a main road. Speedboats are ideal for the emergency rescue services, harbour police, customs officers, and other people who need to travel quickly over short distances.

Houseboat

A houseboat is a floating home. In parts of Asia, houseboats have been used for hundreds of years, many of them never leaving their moorings. Modern houseboats are often fitted with powerful engines and used as holiday homes that travel up and down rivers.

25

Go to Harbour page 30, Travelling on water page 24, Working boats page 28

Ferry

A ferry is a boat that transports people and **vehicles** across a stretch of water. Ferries run in the same way as buses and trains, keeping to the same **routes** and times every day. Most ferries are huge boats that carry hundreds of passengers. During the voyage, passengers leave their cars and relax in lounges and restaurants.

▶ This ferry travels across the sea. It is designed so that vehicles can drive on one end and off the other, without delay.

radar mast
The **radar** lets the crew know how close other ships are and if land is nearby.

bridge
The captain controls the ferry and directs the crew from the bridge.

docking door
At the front and back, there are huge watertight doors. They swing open for vehicles to drive on and off.

propeller
At the front, spinning propellers help the boat to turn. At the back, more propellers drive it forwards.

funnel
A funnel is similar to a giant chimney. It carries away smoke and fumes from the **engines**.

lifeboat
In an emergency, passengers put on life jackets and are lowered into the water in a lifeboat.

Factfile

Seacats, the world's fastest ferries, can travel at 64 km per hour. They speed across the water on two **hulls**.

The right side of a ferry is called port, the left is starboard, the front is the bow and the back is the stern.

In Venice, Italy, ferrymen carry people in boats called gondolas along the city's many **canals**.

passenger deck
On the passenger decks, people eat, relax and visit the shops.

engine
This ferry has two **diesel** engines. They drive the propellers and provide **electricity** for heat and light.

stabilizer
In rough seas, stabilizers help to stop the ship rolling from side to side.

car deck
Vehicles are parked close together on the car **decks**.

Hovercraft
Some ferries, called hovercraft, float along on a cushion of air. Large fans suck the air through a funnel and into a giant rubber base, which keeps the air in place. The hovercraft then rides along quickly just above the surface of the water.

Go to Harbour page 30, Travelling on water page 24, Underwater boats page 32

Working boats

Boats come in many shapes and sizes and each kind is designed to do a particular job. They may fight harbour fires or cut a path through frozen seas so that other boats can pass. The world's largest boats are tankers and container ships. They transport heavy **cargo**, including food, cars and oil, across the ocean to countries on the other side of the world.

Container ship
In the past, goods were loaded on to a ship by hand. This could take up to a week but today a container ship can be loaded in less than 24 hours. Giant metal containers are filled with goods at a factory, then they are taken by lorry or train to the harbour and a crane lowers them into place on the ship. Loading is easy because all the containers are the same size and they stack together like piles of huge bricks.

Supertanker
This supertanker carries oil which has been pumped into its hull through the long pipes on **deck**. Some supertankers are the largest ships ever built — they stretch the length of four football pitches. Once they are moving, it takes several kilometres before they can stop.

crane
Giant cranes lift up to 2,000 containers on to the ship.

hull
First, the containers are stacked inside the ship's **hull**. The extra containers are piled high on the deck.

Fishing trawler

A fishing trawler is designed to stay stable even in rough seas. The crew use special **sonar** equipment to find groups of fish beneath the waves. Then they lower a net into the water to make their catch. When the fish are on board, they are stored in ice to keep them fresh until the trawler reaches the land.

winch
The heavy net is cranked on board using a winch.

fishing net
This fishing net is called a trawl. There are small holes in the net to allow young fish to escape.

Fireboat

A fireboat waits in a harbour or on a city river, in case a blaze breaks out on other boats or in buildings close to the water's edge. Powerful pumps squirt jets of water or foam into a fire to put it out. A fireboat also carries ladders, breathing equipment and first-aid kits to help with rescues and to treat injuries.

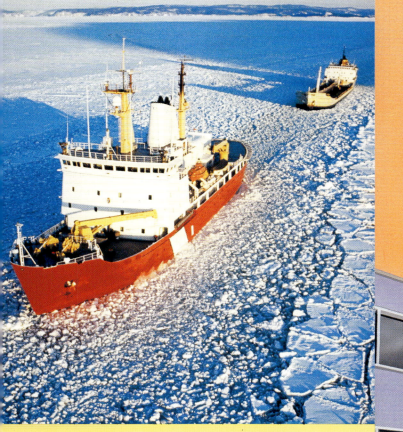

Icebreaker

An icebreaker travels in front of other ships in icy seas. It has a powerful **engine** and an extra-strong hull which breaks up the ice in front, clearing a path for the ships behind. Powerful propellers at both the front and back help the boat to turn or reverse out of the ice.

Go to Ferry page 26, Travelling on water page 24, Working boats page 28

Harbour

A harbour is a calm, sheltered area of water where boats start or end their journeys. Most are natural shelters, where the land curves to make a bay or a wide river joins the sea. A few harbours, built by people, have high stone walls to keep out any rough waves. At a large harbour, ships arrive to pick up **cargo** and drop off passengers.

▶ A busy harbour is full of all kinds of boats, from giant ferries to smaller sailing boats and motorboats.

lighthouse
A flashing lighthouse warns sailors that they are close to land.

buoy
Floating buoys mark out a safe **route** for boats through the water.

dredger
A dredger clears mud from the harbour bottom so that the water remains deep enough for large boats.

marina
After a holiday cruise, owners tie up their motorboats and yachts in the marina.

quay
The quay is a platform where boats are **moored**. A quay that stretches out across the water is called a pier.

ferry terminal
Cars and passengers wait at the terminal before boarding their ferry.

Factfile

Sydney Harbour, in Australia, is the largest natural harbour in the world.

The world's longest pier, at Southend in the UK, stretches for over 2 km. Shops, amusement arcades and even a railway run along its length.

One of the first lighthouses was built over 2,000 years ago in Egypt. It was a wonder of the ancient world.

A tug boat often meets big ships at the entrance to the harbour and guides them safely to the quay. The crew attaches a strong rope and the tug pulls the ship along using its powerful **engines**.

warehouse
Goods are stored in the warehouse before they are loaded on to a cargo ship.

A ship's chandler sells supplies, such as ropes and sails, for small boats. He also sells lifebelts and waterproof clothing, which sailors wear to keep safe and dry.

dry dock
Boats are cleaned and repaired in the dry dock, after the water has been pumped out through a gate.

A coastguard sails around the harbour making sure that everything is in order. She checks that all the boats have the correct safety equipment and watches out for any ships in trouble.

Go to Travelling on water page 24, Working boats page 28

Underwater boats

Most boats float on the top of the water, but a few kinds dive into the depths below. Here they do many jobs, from exploring the sea bottom to searching for shipwrecks or repairing oil rigs. An underwater boat carries air for its crew to breathe. It is also extremely strong to stop it from being crushed by the **pressure**, or push, of the water around it.

▼ This underwater boat, called a submersible, is studying animals and plants on the sea floor.

sonar
Special **sonar** equipment looks out for underwater obstacles, such as mountains or big rocks.

view port
The crew studies the sea floor through the glass view port.

video camera
In dark waters, a special video camera shows the crew what lies nearby.

robot arm
Robot arms collect samples from the sea bottom. They are also useful for carrying out repairs.

sample basket
Samples are put into a basket and studied later.

cabin
Inside the cabin, there are controls for steering the submersible and working the robot arms.

Underwater robots
This submersible is called a ROV which stands for Remote Operated Vehicle. It does not carry a crew and is controlled from a ship above the surface of the ocean.

propeller
A spinning propeller pushes the submersible along.

How a submarine dives

A submarine is used by navies to find and attack ships and other submarines. It has ballast tanks which allow it to dive and surface.

Diving

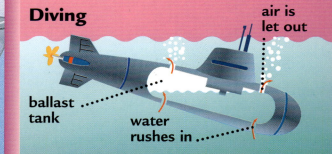

air is let out

ballast tank

water rushes in

1 Air is let out of the ballast tanks and water rushes in. This makes the submarine heavier and it starts to dive.

Surfacing

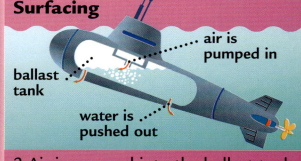

air is pumped in

ballast tank

water is pushed out

2 Air is pumped into the ballast tanks, pushing the water out. The submarine becomes lighter and starts to rise.

ballast tank
These tanks are filled with air or water, to make the submersible move up or down.

Go to Aeroplane page 36, Airport page 40

Travelling in the air

People have always dreamed of flying through the air, but nobody knew how until about 200 years ago. The earliest successful flights took place in hot-air balloons, towards the end of the 18th century. Then, in 1903, Orville Wright became the first pilot to fly a powered aeroplane. It was called The Flyer and flew for just 36 m. Today, aeroplanes fly all over the world, carrying hundreds of passengers at a time.

Hot-air balloon

In 1783, the Montgolfier brothers launched the first passengers in a hot-air balloon. They were a cockerel, a duck and a pig! Today, people ride in balloons for fun. A roaring flame heats the air inside the balloon, making it lighter than the air around it. This makes the balloon rise, lifting the basket off the ground. When it is in the sky, the wind carries the balloon high across the ground.

Airship

An airship is a balloon that has **engines** to drive it forwards. The balloon contains a light **gas**, called helium, so that it can float in the sky. The pilot, who steers the balloon, and a few passengers travel in the small cabin that hangs underneath. Often, airships hover above big sports events so that cameras in the cabin can film the action below.

Glider

A glider is similar to an aeroplane but it does not have an engine. To take off, an aeroplane tows the glider into the sky or a moving car pulls it up on a wire, like a kite, then lets it go. When the glider is in the air, the pilot looks for patches of rising air. The narrow wings catch the rising air, lifting the glider higher.

Float plane

Most aeroplanes need a long runway where they can land, but a float plane can land on a lake, river or the sea. Instead of wheels, it has two large, canoe-like floats that rest on the surface of the water and stop the plane from sinking. This float plane has travelled far out to sea to pick up divers who are carrying out underwater research.

Harrier jump jet

A Harrier is called a jump **jet** because when it takes off, it **launches** straight up into the sky. On each side of the jet, there are two movable tubes, called nozzles. The powerful engine blasts air through these nozzles, pushing up the jet. Jump jets can fly forwards, hover in one place and even go backwards.

cockpit
The tiny cockpit is just big enough for the pilot, who controls the jet.

nozzle
The nozzles swivel to change the direction in which the plane flies.

aircraft carrier
An aircraft carrier is a ship with a runway so that aeroplanes can take off at sea.

Space shuttle

A space shuttle can fly **astronauts** into space and back many times. Two **booster rockets** and three powerful engines blast the shuttle into space, where it travels round the Earth. When the shuttle returns, it glides down to the runway without using any of its engines.

Go to Airport page 40, Helicopter page 38, Travelling in the air page 34

Aeroplane

A modern passenger aeroplane carries hundreds of people all over the world. It travels high above the clouds at more than 800 km per hour. Outside the aeroplane, the air is freezing cold and too thin for people to breathe, but inside the cabin, the passengers can breathe normally. They relax, eat meals, watch films and even make telephone calls as they speed all the way across the world.

wing
The aeroplane's wings are curved on top. Their special shape helps the aeroplane to rise into the air.

flight deck
The captain and the co-pilots take off, fly and land the aeroplane from the flight deck.

galley
In the galley, the cabin crew heat up meals for everyone on board. Trays of food are loaded before take-off.

nose
Inside the nose, there is a weather **radar** which warns the pilot when there is a storm ahead.

engine
This aeroplane is powered by four huge **jet engines**.

Concorde

Concorde is the fastest passenger aeroplane in the world, travelling at more than twice the speed of sound. It carries people over 3,000 km from New York to London in less than three hours.

fin

The fin keeps the aeroplane in a straight line and stops it from rolling from side to side.

rudder

Moving the rudder helps the aeroplane to turn left or right.

cabin

Over 300 passengers can fit into this cabin. They sit upright and fasten their seatbelts for take-off.

On the flight deck

The flight deck is filled with dials, switches and computer screens showing all kinds of flight information. During take-off, the pilot watches his airspeed indicator closely and checks that the runway ahead is clear.

wing flap

The wing flaps move up and down. This helps the aeroplane to lift up during take-off and to brake when it lands.

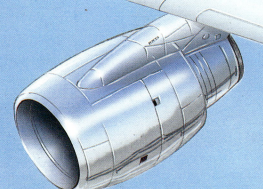

Helicopter

A helicopter is an aircraft with whirling **rotors** which allow it to fly. It cannot travel as fast as most aeroplanes but it moves easily, flying straight up and down, hovering in one spot and even landing in tiny spaces, such as on top of a skyscraper in a busy city. Helicopters do many different jobs, from reporting on traffic conditions to fighting fires and taking people to hospital in an emergency.

▶ This helicopter is rescuing a climber who was stranded on a mountain.

control levers
By moving the control levers, the pilot can make the helicopter fly up and down or backwards and forwards.

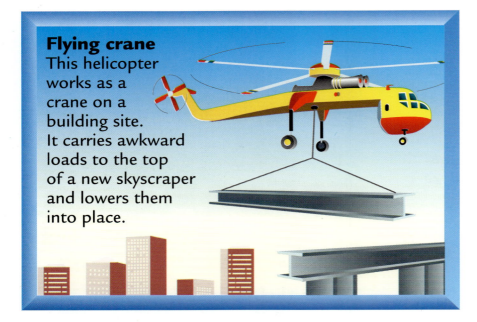

Flying crane
This helicopter works as a crane on a building site. It carries awkward loads to the top of a new skyscraper and lowers them into place.

Crop spraying
Some farmers use helicopters fitted with special equipment to spray their crops with fertiliser or to spread seeds across a field.

Factfile

In 1483, the inventor, Leonardo da Vinci, drew a design for a helicopter but he never built his machine.

The first helicopter that could fly was a model built in 1784. It had two feather rotors to lift it into the air.

In 1989, a helicopter hovered in one spot for over two days. This is the longest hover on record.

main rotor
The main rotor's spinning blades push down the air around them to lift the helicopter into the sky.

tail rotor
The small, upright tail rotor stops the helicopter from spinning round.

winch
A **steel** wire is lowered from a winch to pull up the stranded climber.

safety harness
A strong harness keeps the climber and the rescuer safe.

All at sea
Every few months, this huge helicopter with twin rotors carries workers, equipment and vital food supplies to a stormy oil rig far out at sea. It lands on a small platform called a helipad.

Go to Aeroplane page 36, Emergency vehicles page 18, Travelling in the air page 34

Airport

An international airport is as busy as a small city, with aeroplanes taking off and landing non-stop. Each day, thousands of passengers pass through a large airport and almost as many people work here, from air traffic controllers and customs officers to restaurant staff. Everyone makes sure that the airport runs safely and smoothly.

▼ Teams of people are needed to prepare an aeroplane before take-off.

passenger terminal
Passengers wait inside this building before boarding the aeroplane.

walkway
A covered walkway connects the passenger terminal to the aeroplane.

When you arrive at the airport, you check in. An official takes away heavy luggage for loading on to the aeroplane and gives you a boarding pass.

Next, you walk through a security gate which makes sure that you are not carrying anything dangerous. An X-ray machine checks your bag.

When you are travelling abroad, you need to go to passport control. Here, an official makes sure that your passport is up to date.

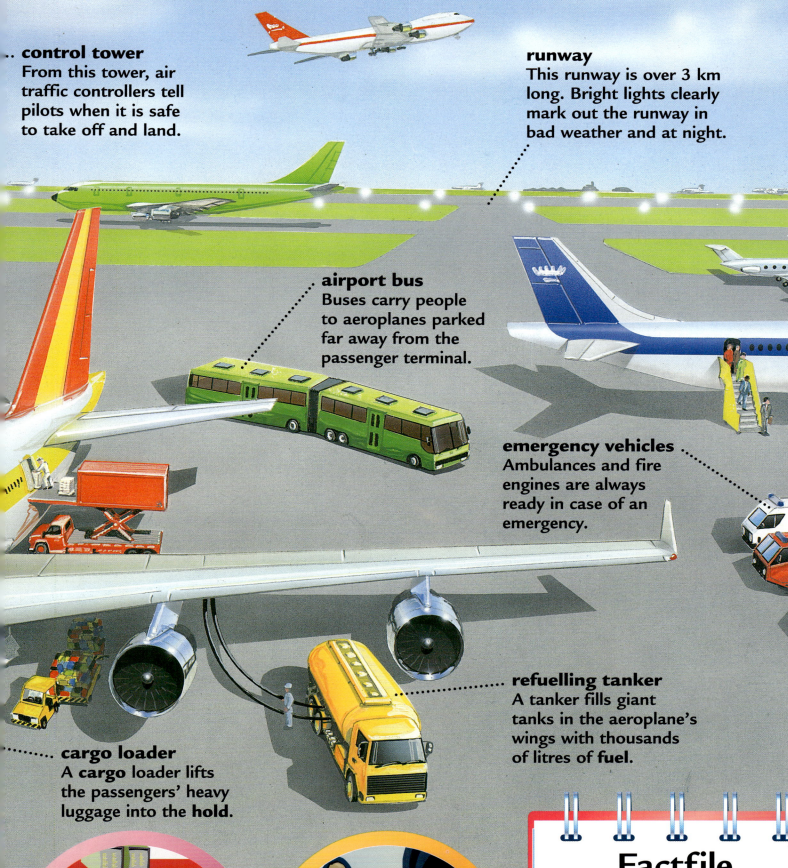

control tower
From this tower, air traffic controllers tell pilots when it is safe to take off and land.

runway
This runway is over 3 km long. Bright lights clearly mark out the runway in bad weather and at night.

airport bus
Buses carry people to aeroplanes parked far away from the passenger terminal.

emergency vehicles
Ambulances and fire engines are always ready in case of an emergency.

refuelling tanker
A tanker fills giant tanks in the aeroplane's wings with thousands of litres of **fuel**.

cargo loader
A **cargo** loader lifts the passengers' heavy luggage into the **hold**.

In the departure lounge, the overhead monitors tell you when your flight is ready to leave. There may be enough time for a snack first.

Finally, you make your way to the boarding gate. Here, the air crew checks your boarding pass before letting you on to the aeroplane. Enjoy your flight!

Factfile

The busiest international airport in the world is Heathrow, London, in the UK. An aeroplane takes off or lands here about every 90 seconds.

In Japan, an entire island had to be built, nearly 5 km out to sea, to make enough space for Kansai International Airport. Roads and high-speed ferries link the airport to the mainland.

Go to Motorcycle page 8, Travelling in the air page 34, Truck page 12

Travelling on snow

When heavy snow falls, **vehicles** with wheels are not much use. The wheels cannot grip the road properly and they sink into the soft snow. People who live in the cold north and explorers often use special vehicles with long, narrow skis instead of wheels. These skis slide smoothly along on top of the snow without sinking.

Ski-plane

A ski-plane has skis attached to its wheels. The wheels help the plane to brake as it lands, while the skis keep it moving in a straight line. In cold places, where roads can be buried under snow for months at a time, ski-planes deliver emergency supplies to local people. The plane needs a smooth surface to land on such as a frozen lake covered with snow.

Snowmobile

A snowmobile is similar to a motorcycle but it moves along on skis and **caterpillar tracks** instead of wheels. A small **engine** drives the tracks while the rider uses the handlebars to turn the skis left or right. Many people who live in the icy north travel by snowmobile because it is a quick way to go from place to place. They can use their vehicles for hunting and fishing trips, for herding reindeer and even for rescuing people in an emergency.

Clearing the roads

Clearing the road after a heavy snowfall, so that cars and trucks can pass by, is a job for a snowblower or a snowplough. This machine is a snowblower. It scoops up the powdery snow in its huge curved blade and then blows it out to one side of the road through a funnel. A snowplough is similar but instead of blowing the snow away it pushes it away with a large blade that is set at an angle.

Skis and snowshoes

Walking across snow is difficult, so people wear skis and snowshoes to help them. In cold countries, many children travel to school on cross-country skis. Snowshoes strap on to the bottom of your boots to make walking much easier.

snowshoes

Snowshoes stop you from sinking into the snow by spreading out your weight over a wide area.

skis
Cross-country skis are long and thin so that they slide along easily. They fix on to the toes of your boots.

Reindeer-sledge

For hundreds of years, sledges have carried people and heavy loads across the freezing snow. The sledges glide along on two curved runners. Teams of reindeer are pulling these sledges but, in some places, husky dogs are used instead.

Amazing facts

On these pages, you can discover amazing facts about all kinds of **vehicles**. You can learn about the biggest and fastest trucks, boats and aeroplanes. You can also find out about strange inventions and what travelling may be like in the future.

How big is it?

Wheely wonder
The Terex Titan is the world's biggest dumper truck. Its giant tyres are as tall as two men.

Amazing wings
The Spruce Goose had the longest wings of any aeroplane. At 97.5 m, they were longer than the Statue of Liberty is tall. It flew only once, in 1947.

Floating giant
The world's longest ship is the supertanker Jahre Viking. It is 458 m long, which is about the length of 15 blue whales.

Strangest transport

People have invented several strange vehicles by mixing up all kinds of odd things!

Pedal power
The Daedalus is a cross between a bicycle and an aeroplane. The pilot pushes the pedals to turn a propeller and move through the air.

Car in a suitcase
This tiny car fits neatly inside a suitcase. When it is not being driven, the owner can fold it away and carry it.

Incredible journeys

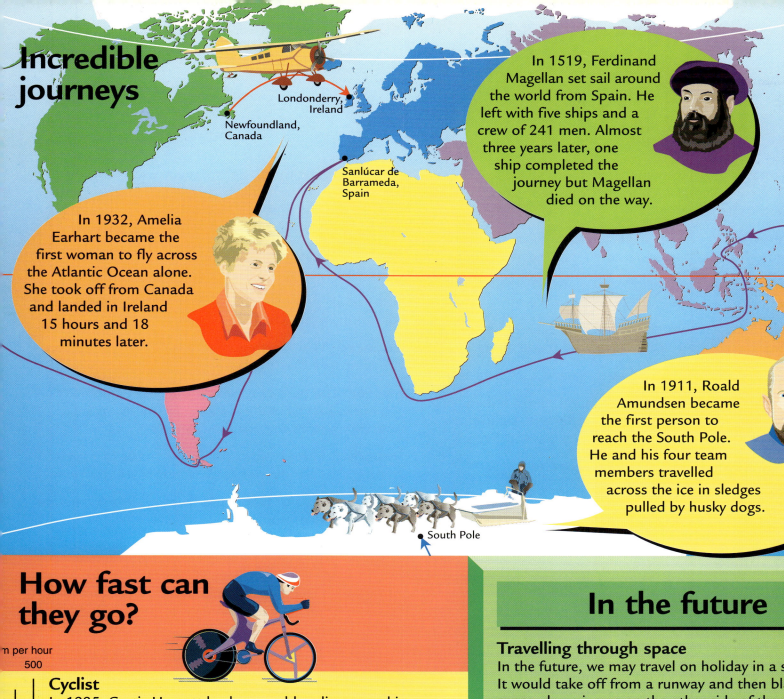

In 1519, Ferdinand Magellan set sail around the world from Spain. He left with five ships and a crew of 241 men. Almost three years later, one ship completed the journey but Magellan died on the way.

In 1932, Amelia Earhart became the first woman to fly across the Atlantic Ocean alone. She took off from Canada and landed in Ireland 15 hours and 18 minutes later.

In 1911, Roald Amundsen became the first person to reach the South Pole. He and his four team members travelled across the ice in sledges pulled by husky dogs.

Londonderry, Ireland

Newfoundland, Canada

Sanlúcar de Barrameda, Spain

South Pole

How fast can they go?

m per hour
500

Cyclist
In 1995, Curtis Harnett broke a world cycling record in a race called the 200 m flying start. He reached a speed of 72 km per hour.

m per hour
500

Boat
In 1978, a boat powered by a **jet engine** broke the water speed record. It travelled at 511 km per hour, over seven times faster than the fastest cyclist.

m per hour
500   1000

Car
In 1997, the Thrust SSC jet car broke the world land speed record. It travelled at 1,227 km per hour, nearly two and a half times faster than the fastest boat.

m per hour
500   1000   1500   2000   2500   3000   3500   4000   4500   5000   5500   6000   6500   7000   7500

Aeroplane
The X-15A-2 rocket plane has flown at 7,274 km per hour, nearly six times as fast as the fastest car.

In the future

Travelling through space
In the future, we may travel on holiday in a spaceplane. It would take off from a runway and then blast into space, dropping us on the other side of the world less than two hours later!

Glossary

astronaut A person who travels into space to explore new places, such as the Moon, or to carry out experiments.

automatic Works by itself. An automatic barrier does not need a person to open it. It opens by itself.

booster rocket A rocket that is attached to a large space rocket to give extra power at take-off.

canal A large channel dug out and filled with water so that barges and other boats can travel along it.

cargo The goods carried by a **vehicle** such as a ship.

caterpillar track A band of metal plates linked together, which **vehicles**, such as diggers, bulldozers and tanks, use instead of wheels to travel off-road.

deck One of the floors on a ship or bus.

diesel A type of **fuel** made from oil. Most trucks and buses run on diesel.

electric Powered by **electricity**.

electricity A type of energy that flows through wires to make **vehicles**, such as trams and some trains, work.

engine The part of a **vehicle** that gives power. The engine of a car burns **fuel** to make it move.

engineer A person who designs, builds or repairs things including **vehicles**, roads and bridges.

fuel A **material** that burns in an **engine** to make it work.

gas A thin substance, such as air, which has no shape and can only be felt if it moves.

gears A set of special toothed wheels. Gears are used to change the speed at which a **vehicle's** wheels turn.

hold The large space inside an aeroplane or ship where luggage or goods are stored.

hull The main part of a ship or boat which sits in the water.

jet The name for an aeroplane powered by jet **engines**. A jet engine works by sucking in air at the front and mixing it with **fuel**. The mixture burns, shooting out hot **gases** at the back.

launch To lift off from the ground. A rocket is launched into space.

material A substance, such as metal, plastic, glass or wood, from which an object is made.

moored When a ship is moored, it is tied up to a quay or to a floating buoy.

motor The part of a **vehicle** that uses **electricity** or burns **fuel** to make it move. Many trains have **electric** motors to turn their wheels.

muscles Parts inside your body, made of tough tissue, that shrink and relax to allow you to move.

petrol A type of **fuel** made from oil. Most cars and motorcycles run on petrol.

pollute To give out or leave behind waste that damages the air, sea or land.

pressure The push or force which an object feels from another object or when it is surrounded by water or **gas**.

radar Equipment that uses radio waves to spot objects out of view. Aeroplanes and ships use radar to spot mountains, storms and other aeroplanes.

robot A machine, controlled by a computer, which often does a job that a person would normally do.

rotor The spinning blades that lift a helicopter into the air.

route The path taken from one place to another. Buses follow the same route each day.

sonar Equipment that uses sound to track underwater objects out of view. Ships use sonar to track icebergs, mountains and shipwrecks.

spacecraft A **vehicle**, such as a space shuttle, that flies in space, circling the Earth or visiting other planets.

steel A strong metal made mostly of iron that is often used to make cars and ships.

streamlined Having a smooth shape which cuts easily through air or water.

submarine A ship that travels underwater.

vehicle A machine for carrying people and goods. Bicycles, cars, trains, ships and aeroplanes are all vehicles.

Index

Accelerator pedal 10
accident 19
aeroplane 4, 5, 25, 34, 35, 36-37, 40, 41, 42, 44, 45
air traffic controller 40, 41
air travel 4, 5, 34-41, 42, 44, 45
aircraft carrier 35
airport 40-41
airship 34
ambulance 19, 41
Amundsen, Roald 45
arrival display 22
articulated truck 12
astronaut 5, 35
Australia 12, 31
automatic door 16, 23

Ballast tank 33
balloon 4, 34
barrier 22
bell 16
Benz, Karl 5
bicycle 4, 6-7, 44
boat 4, 19, 24-33, 35, 44, 45
boot of a car 11
brake pedal 10
brake 6, 10
breakdown truck 19
bridge 15
bridge of a ferry 26
building site 12, 38
buoy 30
bus 4, 5, 16-17, 41
bus station 16
bypass 15

Cab 12, 16, 20, 23
cabin 32, 34, 36, 37
cable, overhead 17, 20
camel 4
Canada 45
canal 27
captain 26, 36
car 4, 5, 10-11, 14, 15, 19, 27, 28, 31, 43, 44, 45
car deck 27
cargo 24, 28, 30, 41

cargo loader 41
cargo ship 24, 31
cart 4
caterpillar tracks 13, 42
cats'-eyes 14
cement truck 13
chandler 31
China 25
coastguard 31
cockpit 35
Concorde 37
container ship 28
control lever 38
control room 23
crane 28, 38
crew 5, 24, 26, 31, 32, 36
crop spraying 38
cycle 6-7, 45

Daedalus 44
Daimler, Gottfried 9
dashboard 10
desert 4
destination plate 17
diesel 12, 16, 20, 24, 27
diesel-electric train 20
digger 13
docking door 26
dog 43, 45
door 16, 22, 26
double-decker bus 16
dredger 30
driver 7, 10, 12, 13, 14, 16, 19, 20, 23
driver's cab 12, 20, 23
dry dock 31
dumper truck 44

Earhart, Amelia 45
Egypt, Ancient 4, 31
electricity 10, 16, 17, 20, 22, 27
emergency handle 21
emergency vehicle 18-19, 38, 41, 42
engine 5, 6, 8, 9, 10, 11, 12, 16, 24, 25, 27, 29, 31, 34, 35, 36, 42, 45
escalator 23
exhaust 11

Farmer 38
ferry 26-27, 30, 31, 41
ferry terminal 31
fin of an aeroplane 37
fireboat 29
fire engine 18, 41
fishing net 29
fishing trawler 29
flight deck 36, 37
float plane 35
Flyer, The 5, 34
flyover 15
fork-lift truck 13
frame of a bicycle 6
frame of a motorcycle 8
France 15
fuel 9, 16, 41
fuel tank 9
funnel 27, 43

Galley 36
gas 11, 34
gear 6, 9
gear lever 9
glider 34
Golden Gate Bridge 15
gondola 27
Grand Central Station 21

Handlebars 6, 7, 42
harbour 28, 29, 30-31
hard shoulder 14
Harnet, Chris 45
Harrier jump jet 35
headlamp 8, 14
Heathrow Airport 41
helicopter 38-39
helipad 39
helium 34
helmet 6, 7, 8
hold of an aeroplane 41
hot-air balloon 4, 34
houseboat 25
hovercraft 27
hovering 35, 38
hull 25, 27, 28, 29
husky dog 43, 45

Icebreaker 29
indicator light 11
inspector 21
Ireland 45

Jahre Viking 44
Japan 23, 41
jet car 45
jet engine 36, 45
jump jet 35
junction 15

Kansai International Airport 41
Kudo, Yasuyuki 9

Ladder 18, 29
lane 14
Leonardo da Vinci 38
life jacket 24, 27
lifebelt 19, 31
lifeboat 19, 27
light 8, 11, 14, 17, 18, 19
lighthouse 30, 31
liner 25, 33
loader 13
locomotive 20
London 16, 22, 25, 37, 41
luggage 11, 40, 41
Lyon 15

Magellan, Ferdinand 45
maglev train 21
map 23
marina 30
mast 24, 26
mirror 9
Montgolfier, Joseph
  and Jacques 4, 34
Moon 5, 11
Moscow 21
motor, electric 20
motor scooter 8
motorboat 30
motorcycle 8-9, 42
motorway 14, 42
mountain bicycle 6
mountain rescue 38-39
muscle 6

Net, fishing 29
New York 21, 22, 25, 37
nozzle 35

Ocean liner 25, 33
oil 28
outrigger leg 18
ox cart 4

Pallet 13
pannier 9
pantograph 17, 20
Paris 22
passenger 4, 10, 16, 20,
  21, 22, 23, 24, 25, 26,
  27, 30, 31, 34, 36, 37,
  40, 41
passenger terminal 40, 41
passport 40
pedal of a bicycle 6
petrol 5, 9, 10, 12
pier 30, 31
pilot 34, 35, 36, 37,
  41, 44
police car 19
pollution 5, 6, 10, 17
power car 20
pressure 32
propeller 26, 27, 29,
  33, 44

Quay 30, 31

Racing bicycle 7
radar 26, 36
radio 19, 20
railway 12, 15, 20, 21,
  22, 23, 31
reed boat 24
refuse truck 13
reindeer 42, 43
Remote Operated Vehicle
  see ROV
rickshaw 7
road 7, 8, 12, 13, 14-15,
  16, 17, 41, 42, 43
road train 12
robot 11, 33
rocket 5, 35
rollerblades 7
rotor 38, 39
route 16, 23, 26, 30
ROV 33
rubber 6, 27
rudder 24, 37
runway 37, 41
Russia 5, 21

Safety cage 18
safety harness 39
sail 4, 24, 31
sailing boat 4, 24, 30
school bus 17
Scotland 6
Seacat 27
seatbelt 10
ship see boat
sign 14
siren 18
skateboarding 7
ski 42, 43
ski-plane 42
sledge 43, 45
sleeper 21
slip road 14
snow 42, 43
snowblower 43
snowmobile 42
snowplough 43
snowshoe 43
solar car 10
sonar 29, 32
space shuttle 5, 35
spacecraft 5
spaceplane 45
Spaghetti Junction 15
speedboat 25
Spruce Goose 44

stabilizer 27
station 16, 20, 21, 22, 23
steam train 4
steel 6, 17, 39
steering wheel 10
Stephenson, George 4
streamlining 7, 8
stretch limousine 11
submarine 33
submersible 32-33
Sumerians 4
supertanker 28, 44
Sydney Harbour 31

Tail rotor 39
tanker 28, 41
Terex Titan 44
Thames, River 33
Thrust SSC jet car 45
ticket inspector 21
ticket machine 16, 22
Titanic 33
Titicaca, Lake 24
Tokyo 23
tractor 12
traffic jam 5, 7, 8, 10, 15
traffic light 14
trail bike 8
trailer 12
train 4, 20-23, 28
tram 16, 17
Trans-Siberian Railway 21
trawler 29
tread 8
truck 12-13, 19, 43
tug boat 31
tunnel 15, 22
turntable 18
tyre 6, 7, 8, 13, 44

UK 15, 31, 33, 41
underground train 22-23
underwater boat 32-33
USA 5, 15, 21, 45

Van 5
vehicle 5, 6, 9, 12, 14, 18,
  19, 26, 27, 42, 41, 44
Venice 27
video 23, 32

view port 32
Vinci, Leonardo da see
  Leonardo da Vinci
Vladivostok 21
Volkswagen Beetle 11
voltage 20

Walkway 40
warehouse 13, 31
water transport 4, 24-33,
  35, 44, 45
wheel 4, 6, 7, 8, 9, 10,
  11, 12, 21, 42
winch 29, 39
windscreen 8
wing flap 37
wing mirror 9
wing of an aeroplane 34,
  36, 37, 44
working boat 28-29
Wright, Orville 5, 34
Wright, Wilbur 5

X-15A-2 rocket plane 45

Yacht 24, 30

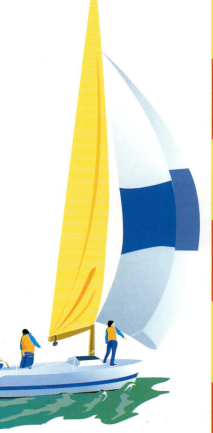